Lifeline

LIFELINE

A Parent's Guide to Coping
with a Child's Serious or
Life-Threatening Medical Issue

Dr. Denise Morett

NEW YORK

NASHVILLE • MELBOURNE • VANCOUVER

LIFELINE

A Parent's Guide to Coping with a Child's Serious or Life-Threatening Medical Issue

Published in New York, New York, by Morgan James Publishing in partnership with Difference Press. Morgan James is a trademark of Morgan James, LLC. www.MorganJamesPublishing.com

The Morgan James Speakers Group can bring authors to your live event. For more information or to book an event visit The Morgan James Speakers Group at www.TheMorganJamesSpeakersGroup.com.

Neither the author nor the publisher assumes any responsibility for errors, omissions, or contrary interpretations of the subject matter herein. Any perceived slight of any individual or organization is purely unintentional.

This book is not intended as a substitute for the medical advice of physicians or other counselor professionals. The reader should regularly consult a physician or relevant professional in matters relating to his/her health and particularly with respect to any symptoms that may require diagnosis or medical attention, health or alternative healing.

ISBN 9781683504146 paperback
ISBN 9781683504153 eBook
Library of Congress Control Number: 2017901033

Cover Design by:
John Weber
john@jwebercreative.com

Interior Design by:
Chris Treccani
www.3dogdesign.net

In an effort to support local communities, raise awareness and funds, Morgan James Publishing donates a percentage of all book sales for the life of each book to Habitat for Humanity Peninsula and Greater Williamsburg.

Get involved today! Visit
www.MorganJamesBuilds.com

Dedication

For my son, Ryan.

You bravely face life-changing challenges and keep going when many of us would feel like giving up. Your spirit and perseverance give me the courage to keep going at times I have felt collapse was near. Thank you, my amazing young son, for all you bring to my life and the gifts you are giving the world. If it were not for you, I would not have become a parent and this book would never have been written.

Table of Contents

Introduction

"I feel like I'm on a crazy ride on a new planet with unending waves crashing all around me. I feel like I'm drowning in the swirling sea."

- Parent of a child with a serious medical issue

f you're reading this book, then you have a child with a serious or life-threatening medical issue. There are no words that can fully capture how truly awful this is for you and your child. The level of despair, desperation, and constant worry for your child's life are likely beyond anything you could have imagined. For parents whose children are ill, injured, or suffering, emotions run high, and thoughts can feel circular and even extreme. The level of panic is typically at a tsunami level. If you're like me (I'll tell you my story in a minute), it all seems surreal.

I am so truly sorry this is happening in your life. No parent or child should ever experience such a thing. Nothing seems right when there is something wrong with your child. It's like being on another planet.

Perhaps your child has been diagnosed with a serious and/or life-threatening condition. Perhaps your child was injured in an accident or hurt suddenly, placing your child's life at risk. Perhaps your child has an ongoing chronic condition that will present lifelong challenges and unique needs for your child. Perhaps your child needs serious or life-threatening surgery.

When under such unimaginable stress, you experience many unexpected and extreme thoughts and emotions, from shock and fear to anger, hopelessness, and helplessness. Your thoughts are racing as you try, over and over, to figure out the biggest and the smallest details and issues. There's little relief, and little sleep. Managing your home, job, other children, your child's school issues, and, likely, many aspects of your "regular" life is all overwhelming–especially while you are trying to negotiate the medical world, treatment facilities, hospital stays, insurance, and medications. What if there were some things you could do that would actually help?

It might seem ridiculous and even impossible that much of anything will help right now. But even with all the worry, stress, and endless challenges, it is possible to have moments of relaxation and peace, find effective coping strategies and tips, and avoid the long-term effects of stress and strain. Even when there is "no time," you can have restorative, restful moments that truly can help you survive and actually thrive when under the worst of circumstances. You can actually choose how you respond to what's happening.

Most likely, you have put off or have not even considered some or most of your own needs. That is totally expected and normal when a child has a medical issue. Even when everything's fine, parents tend to put themselves second. But in the midst of crisis, taking time for self-care, let alone pleasure, can feel inappropriate, challenging, and maybe even impossible.

So, the fact that you are reading this book at this moment is a feat of accomplishment in and of itself.

Typical stress management techniques and strategies may not work or be practical. But finding effective, simple, and helpful strategies is so important, particularly when time may be limited.

That's part of why I wrote this book. I want you to have simple, easy, and effective resources that may not be otherwise readily available. My hope is for at least one easier moment in your life, for one thing that can go more smoothly. I also want you to know that peace and ease, even now, is possible. With the right resources, you can find empowerment and strength to support and guide you at all times.

If there's one thing I could give you from this book, it would be this:

It is okay not to be okay! And yet, you can also be okay when everything is not okay.

What I mean is that you do not have to figure it all out and have everything be resolved to feel okay. You can acknowledge and be aware your experiences. You can have moments of peace and balance that will actually support you so you can be with your child's circumstances and your experiences in the best way possible. Most of all, you can know that there is no right or wrong way to do this. Please don't judge yourself.

You may find it next to impossible to believe you can feel peace and a sense of "okayness" among the swirling sea of stress. But finding even the smallest sense of some peace will give you a little space and help you manage and take care of yourself and your child. When a space is created that allows for all your experiences, okay and not okay, it will help you cope with the actual stress.

As a clinical psychologist, I have worked for over 25 years with many individuals and families. Many of my patients have had a family member with a life-threatening medical issue. I have witnessed the complete desperation and despair. The space I provided for my patients in order to listen to their experience seemed to help.

For most of those years, I worked with families facing medical issues with a compassionate but nonetheless intellectual understanding of their challenges. Then, in 2014, my entire life changed. I was met with the most extreme and stressful life-changing challenge of my life. My then 14 year-old son was diagnosed with a rare, life-threatening form of cancer.

It turned my life upside down. I found myself on the other side of the desk, not just imagining and hearing about the shock and pain, but experiencing it myself. I was the one in despair, devastated and in near-collapse. It felt everything in my life had stopped and I was in constant survival mode.

I saw firsthand how overwhelming it is to deal with the healthcare and medical treatment system, and to negotiate all of it while in a complete state of panic and in adrenaline-driven-survivor mode. Somehow I managed. I was worn out and barely functioning at times, but somehow, I went on. It took a huge toll on my health and wellbeing.

My son's illness continued for an extended time, throwing our family into an ongoing crisis. His life was at risk and the future was uncertain. Like you, I could not imagine how I was going to continue to help my son through his challenges or how I would manage. I worried and feared for his life. I kept thinking there should be more support and help for him and for me as his parent. I kept feeling surprised that people did not get how challenging our life had become.

I had no time for support groups, and even if I had, there didn't seem to be any that were relevant. I kept feeling a sense of being lost without anything to hold onto to support me or my family. Despite knowing in my head that I was not crazy, I did have the experience of feeling totally crazy at times. I felt that little was validating my experience and almost nobody could listen to my experience. Somehow I managed and I did eventually find things to hold me up and support me. It was not easy and not readily available. I kept saying and thinking there should be simple, easy-to-find support for children and families dealing with such circumstances.

That is why I wrote this book. To provide space, validation, tips, and techniques that actually make a difference in how you function and experience the circumstances and your child's medical issues. I wrote this book to provide a lifeline of sorts when there seems to be nothing much to hold onto. My goal and greatest wish with this book is to provide some help to you as a parent when little or nothing may seem to help. When nobody seems to actually relate to or get your experience. I developed some unique coping strategies and my L.I.F.E. breathing approach (more on that in chapter 1). Through these, I found that I could find peace and restorative moments where I did not think there were any possible. I've seen patients and other parents benefit from my approaches, even when there did not seem to be any possible sign of peace or comfort.

The chapters that follow can be read in any order you desire. The L.I.F.E. breathing strategy approach is outlined in the first chapter, which describes the unique stress parents are under. The second chapter is about restfulness and finding peace despite the stress. The third chapter is about overall wellness strategies. The fourth chapter addresses issues dealing with medical settings and situations. The fifth chapter deals with issues related to changing social connections. The sixth chapter focuses on some changes in the child. The seventh chapter is about some changes in the family. The eighth chapter is about transforming beyond trauma. There are also useful appendices at the back of the book for your reference.

Throughout the book, you'll find imagery, meditations, and exercises along with some tips/strategies that you can use. These can be tailored and changed to fit your life and what works for you. If you want, email me at DrMorett@valstar.net and I'll help you customize your own version of the suggestions and imagery exercises and meditations.

You can also check out the LIFELINE page on my website (parentingchildwithmedicalissues.com) and my Facebook page

(@parentsofchildrenwithlifethreateningmedicalissue), where I've posted helpful information and support.

Please also see the appendices at the end of this book for techniques and strategies for stress management and a wish list of what you may want from others while dealing with your child's medical issues.

When I look back, I recall saying to myself that I needed a lifeline to hold onto to support me. I would say, "Someone please throw me a lifeline here!" The idea and title of the book reflects that sentiment. Lifelines save and support us when we need them most.

LIFELINE was written to help when nothing may seem to help. It is written to be simple and accessible. All the tips and techniques were designed to be easy and quick to use. As I've said, and will say more than once in this book: there is no right or wrong way to deal with crisis and stress. There are no rules. Anything positive you can do that results in some comfort and peace is the right thing for you. Please use this book in any way that works for you.

CHAPTER 1

Your Unique Stress and What to Do About It

"Life isn't about waiting for the storm to pass... It's about learning to dance in the rain."
-Vivian Greene

'm sure you recall that moment when everything changed due to your child's medical issue. Time slowed down – or even sped up. Everything seemed surreal. There is no anguish and experience that can compare to learning there is something wrong and your child's life is at risk. It's a traumatic event like no other.

After many months of what we were told were my 14-year-old son's unresolved colds and allergies, I came home one day to him pointing out that he had a bump on his face. We had been going to the doctor for over a year with little to no resolution of his symptoms. With the appearance of this bump, we headed back to the doctor's office.

Our family physician and I agreed that it appeared to be an easy-to-resolve polyp that a specialist could diagnose and remove. A polyp diagnosis fit with all the symptoms. Finally we would have some resolution and my son would have relief!

I was a little stressed out by having to go for yet another medical office visit, even one that appeared to be minor. I really hated dealing with any health issue with my child. He was not pleasant in doctors' offices and rarely cooperated with exams. I was worried that he would get upset about being examined and wondered how he would cope with having a medical procedure.

I will never forget the look on the specialist's face when he diagnosed my son. The color drained from his face as he pushed his chair away after looking in my son's nose. It was not a nasal polyp. It was a tumor.

I could not feel myself in that moment. I recall looking at my son and feeling complete terror, followed by a rush of adrenaline as I caught myself and changed my expression to one of, "We will do what we need to do." I had to reassure my son, who looked lost and terrified. I went into crisis mode – like parents do – and immediately rallied to cope and take care of him and the situation.

It got worse. On the phone with the doctor later that day, I asked if my child could die. He had called to confirm the presence of a large tumor that had infiltrated the base of my son's skull – my son's skull! – and a large portion of his entire internal facial cavities. "Please be straight with me," I begged the doctor. "Can my son die from this?"

His reply of "yes" immediately took me off this planet. Again, I could barely feel my body – but I didn't have to. I was going to do what was needed and focus only on my child. I didn't matter in that moment. My needs were not present.

Later that night, I lay in bed staring at the ceiling. I could not stop my brain from scrambling around and sleep was impossible. I felt paralyzed. I knew I should try to get some rest so I could handle seeing patients the next day while unbelievably stressed, but I had no idea how to help myself when I didn't even feel connected to myself.

As it turned out, I forgot to think of myself for a long, long time. It was not until months later that I started to sense my own needs and began to feel the effects of that ongoing stress.

I wish that I could go back to that first night and have a good long talk with myself. I would have saved myself from any unnecessary drain of my energy, because I was going to need it all later. I would say some helpful, loving, and kind words like: "Breathe. Yes, this is terrifying and awful. But you're a loving, capable, and very courageous person and mom. You will get through this one step at a time. You can trust the universe, spirit, God, or whatever positive energy exists. It is there supporting you at all times. Please stop blaming and judging yourself. Please be kind to yourself. You need all that positive energy now." Those kind words would have helped.

And it's because of this – those words I wish I could go back and tell myself when we were in crisis – that I am writing this book to you. Because I can't reach back in time and tell me how to take care of myself – but I can tell you. I can pass along the basics of self-care I wish I had known then. About breathing, not judging; about giving space and validating your experiences; about taking breaks from the stress whenever you can by choosing positive/empowered images and focus; and about how to support your own health and wellbeing while doing what you can to minimize the effects of long-term stress.

The typical strategies for stress management may not work or even occur to you. You may not even want to bother. All that may get lost, and *you* may feel lost. Prolonged medical challenges with ongoing issues and treatments can create chronic stress, with all the accompanying consequences of that stress.

In the introduction of this book, I mentioned my quick L.I.F.E. breathing technique. I developed it as a way to remember to breathe and engage in self-care at a time when it seemed nearly impossible to cope. I found myself saying to myself, "Recall L.I.F.E.," and then I would practice the breathing. The goal, at a minimum, was not to collapse. This helps. Breathing helps. Do it all day. Keep breathing to support yourself and maximize your strength.

L.I.F.E. = **Love**
Inhale
Flowing
Exhale

L.I.F.E.: A Quick Strategy for Immediate Calm and Self-Support

Step One - **L**ove: Focus on the love of your child and yourself.

Step Two - **I**nhale: Breathe in through your nose slowly for five seconds.

Step Three - **F**lowing: Focus on thoughts and images of flowing and freedom.

Step Four - **E**xhale: Breathe out through your nose slowly for eight seconds.

Try this for three consecutive breaths. Try pausing for two seconds between the in breath and out breath. Remember **L.I.F.E.** when you are stressed out by your child's medical issues.

I found that keeping these concepts on hand and close by for reference helped me and has helped many other parents remember to tap into a greater source of strength. As I continually find myself saying, there aren't any right or wrong ways of coping and there are no rules here. Do what works for you and your family!

Practice

So perhaps take a moment now to breathe. Use the L.I.F.E. strategy and breathe in a way that supports you. Now you can add this next step: Say some nice, kind, and loving words to yourself. You are strong. You are loving. You are courageous. Breathe in those words. Practice saying those words. You might even want to write these words down now.

CHAPTER 2

Rest and Relax
in the Face of Stress

"You can't stop the waves, but you can learn to surf."
– Jon Kabat-Zinn

The stress of your child's medical issue is all-consuming. I wasn't able to think or feel much of anything else, and I was like that for months and months. I tried to focus on other parts of life, but I was mostly consumed by my son's health crisis. I see now that I could have taken mental breaks and focused on restorative moments and energy. I see that I did not take these restorative breaks because I was just in survival mode pretty much all the time. I think I believed on some level that if I stopped thinking about my son's illness and pressed pause on my constant immersion in problem-solving, I was somehow not helping him. I was terrified to let go.

My pre-occupation and obsession with our circumstances was totally normal and expected, but looking back, I see how I could have paused that mode of survival and total absorption and inserted some peace and calm. I see how I could have avoided getting so worn out and run down. I see how I exhausted myself. Now, I see and know that I could have avoided some of the long-term psychological and physiological fatigue that resulted from my not allowing myself to take a break.

Imagine that it's possible to actually find some peace in the midst of overwhelming and draining stress. It's possible without attending a yoga class, having a massage, sitting for a meditation, or anything else that you may not have the time, money, or energy to do at this moment in time. You can sleep and get the rest you need to take care of your child, your family, and yourself. You could be connected to energy that supports and renews at a time when there doesn't seem to be anything to hold onto.

If you're like I was, you are overwhelmed with all that is happening. I can recall describing the experience as being like huge waves that kept hitting me and knocking me over. I would barely get up from one challenge when the next one would hit. I struggled for air again and again. How do you find a way to "surf' when the waves are continual and perhaps even bigger with each passing day?

Here's how: you can find some relief in moments that you may not think exist. Actually create moments of time, space, and peace for yourself out of seemingly nothing at all. It may sound a little strange and even impossible, this idea of creating space and helpful energy where it doesn't seem to exist and when there seems to be no time to look. But you can find these moments while in the shower, brushing your teeth, using the bathroom, or driving to and from work or the hospital as a time for renewal and support. Those are often the times and moments that we problem-solve and plan, which is normal and extremely useful, particularly during high stress and chronic stress. But we can get lost in thought. We can use some of those moments in supportive ways, too.

You can try taking even one of those moments, for a short time, even for as little as 30 seconds, to restore and rest. You can picture a pleasing image. You can be present in the actual moment by feeling your body sitting or standing in your space. You can even use some moments of waiting in a medical setting or sitting with your child that can also be restorative despite the worry and stress. You can shift or soften your focus, even a little, and find small, powerful islands of energy and support.

Connected to Energy Exercise

Imagine an anchor line that you can send from your body into the core of the earth and that will keep you grounded. Imagine there is another line linking you to the energy and power of the universe above. Imagine you could even follow that line up and out into the universe, and look down at the earth while connecting with the energy of the universe beyond our planet. You can use that energy coming into your body to support you from above the planet while also connecting to the energy of the anchor that is in the core of the earth below. Try imagining this for even a brief moment. This energy line you created by connecting you to the core of the earth below and the universe above can be your own personal lifeline. You can keep this line of support running through you. It is there to support you. You can do this anytime and anywhere.

The Big Picture Approach

It's very helpful to balance and see all parts of your life, not just the time you spend in medical settings. Being in all aspects of your days and finding the times that are not about your child's medical issues. You do not have to live in a constant state of stress and survival.

The point I'm making here it that it's perfectly alright and helpful to not live in the constant crisis every waking (and sleeping) moment of your days.

Another way to cope and achieve some balance can be choosing to shift your perspective and beliefs. For example, I never said, "My son's tumor." I didn't want that thing to be owned by or belong to him. Drawing this boundary on our language helped me maintain an affirming belief and perspective. I kept saying, "We are dealing with a stressful situation, but *we are not* the stressful situation. We are not defined by it. My son is not defined by the tumor." Even though our circumstances were life-changing, my son and our lives were not totally about the disease. I do believe it is possible to have a moment of a larger perspective at times. Imagine you can see the totality of your life and your child's existence. The medical issue is only a part of life.

Now, there is a double-edged sword here I want to caution you about. I fully believe that it is vital to coping that you see the reality of the medical issue and how awful and terrible it is for your child, you, and your family. It's crucial that there be nothing dismissive at all that minimizes the severity of the circumstances. It is important that you are validated. It really is as bad as it is. You're not exaggerating.

But you can also focus on what else is going on in life, and on other aspects of your child. I recall one of my patients, a parent, asking to speak about other things: "Please, please, let's just talk about my child's beautiful eye color. My child is not his disease."

Sleep

Sleep is likely one of the biggest challenges for you when something is wrong with your child. How can you cope with the unimaginable stress of the circumstances, never mind relax enough to get some sleep? To sleep, we have to let go on many levels. You may have trouble getting to sleep or, if you can fall asleep, you may wake up and not be able to get back to sleep. In the quiet of the night is often when fears and obsessive thoughts occur. In the small hours, worries and fears may seem worse, and it's not unusual for them to jolt you awake or keep you awake.

Several strategies can help promote the sleep that's so necessary for your own health so that you can be at your best to care for your child and family. It's okay to sleep. It's okay to let go for the night and rest. Tell that part of your brain that it can take a break from problem-solving and trust that sleep will help with it all.

To fall asleep, try the L.I.F.E breathing technique or any way that helps you take a few deep breaths, and let the stress leave your body. You can notice the points in your body that are tense and try to let that tension go. You can imagine you are in a peaceful place – perhaps a beach or forest – with soothing light and energy. You can imagine whatever place you like. Enjoy that image and place even if there are upsetting thoughts and you get distracted. It's alright; you can keep imagining the place of peace, too. There is room for it all. Imagine a calming sun or light that lets you slip away for a restful sleep. Imagine that the light supports and holds you while you rest and envelops you and your family. Whatever sleep you get will be restful and restorative.

You can also try playing some restful, sleep-promoting music. There are lots of recordings of music that are available and easy to access online. Playing music may help particularly if you need something to occupy your mind and the sleep imagery above is not working or a fit for you to try. If you have a favorite classical piece of music, you can try that for background sleep music.

Sometimes I find some music helpful and at other times I find it annoying. Sometimes the sounds of nature can be helpful and a fit. Sometimes, they're annoying, too. It really depends on personal preference – and your preferences can shift by the day and the moment. I find that trying out different music is the best way to find the fit for the moment. Try going on YouTube and searching for "sleep music." Lots of choices will come up to try. If you want a shorter piece (45 minutes or so), you can try "Sleep Music Delta Waves: Relaxing Music to Help you Sleep, Deep Sleep, Inner Peace (45 min)." An example of a longer option for continual music while you sleep is this eight-hour version "8 HOUR Sleep Music Delta Waves: Relaxing Music, Beat Insomnia, Calming Music, Deep Sleep." Explore and experiment with what works for you. As an aside, your child may also benefit from some of the same kind of music to calm and help him or her sleep as well.

There are also many healthy, non-narcotic sleep aids that can be used to support your physiological process of sleep. Oral magnesium, taken at bedtime, is one of them. You can alternatively soak in an Epsom salt bath, which is a way to absorb magnesium into your body through your skin while it also helps soothe muscle tension. Magnesium is helpful for supporting your immune system as well as restoring daily energy levels. It promotes sleep and reduces anxiety and symptoms of emotional upset.

Using essential oils can also help with sleep. Putting lavender oil on your pillow or on a cloth near your head will promote relaxation and induce a state of calm and sleep. Lavender is easy to find at natural groceries and pharmacies, and easy to carry with you for its calming effect. You can also check the LIFELINE website (parentingchildwithmedicalissues.com) for specific strategies.

I also find that applying pressure or gentle massage to specific acupressure points will help with sleep and reduce stress throughout the day. There are many easily accessible articles online as well as You Tube videos demonstrating acupressure points for sleep. One example I find helpful is to apply gentle pressure and massage to the area right in the middle of your eyebrows. Gently applying pressure to and massaging this area for just a few moments is known to reduce anxiety, relieve panic, alleviate fears, counteract depression, and promote sleep. The outer ear and ear lobe is another area to which to apply acupressure and gentle massage in order to promote sleep.

Adrenal Fatigue: What It Is and How to Deal with It

When you are in survival mode and under constant and/or chronic stress, there is a surge and constant flow of high levels of adrenaline from the two tiny glands known as your adrenals. It is easy for the adrenals to get overused and to tip over into "adrenal fatigue." I wish I had known as much as I do now about adrenal fatigue. I didn't realize there were things I could do to support my body and avoid extreme adrenal fatigue. These include getting sleep, taking adrenal support formulas (check health food stores and online), and eating fermented foods (kombucha and raw sauerkraut, for instance).

Taking rescue remedies, mentioned both on the LIFELINE page of my website and also in Appendix I. Using remedies throughout the day and at the highest times of stress will not only support you when under stress, but will also help you avoid adrenal fatigue and the long-term complications of stress.

Compassion Fatigue and How to Deal with It

Taking care of your child and family can be extremely stressful under normal circumstances, never mind when there is a serious or life-threatening medical issue. Most likely you are consumed by worry and want to protect your child. You may find that at least at first, you have seemingly unending levels of compassion. But at some point, you may notice a variation or shift.

I remember becoming so exhausted and overwhelmed that I practically shut down, even shutting out my child's crying. I really judged myself for that. How could I feel nothing when my child was fighting for his life? I actually experienced agitation, anger, numbness, and irritation. I had moments of thinking to myself, "Oh, I wish he would just go to sleep and stop complaining." I thought that I must be a terrible mother, and that I was failing my child. How could I think that way and feel these feelings?

The answer is what's called "compassion fatigue." There was nothing wrong with me. It's normal to shut down because we feel so *much* compassion and we are exhausted and stressed from the intensity of taking care of someone who has a serious or life-threatening medical issue.

There is nothing wrong with you if you have this experience. It is a form of protection, actually. When we are overloaded, we shut down as a means to avoid collapse. It's actually helpful. I did not need to judge myself, just as you don't need to judge yourself. I was not a horrible mother. I was a stressed out, compassion-fatigued, adrenal-fatigued mother. It was understandable given the hardship we were enduring. Judging yourself for those experiences, feelings, and thoughts just adds further stress and damage. It does you no good to sit in judgment of yourself.

When I was in the pediatric ICU with my son, I witnessed many parents and families dealing with a child with a life-threatening illness. The ICU was an open unit with four patients to a room, separated only by curtains. We saw many families engaged in their own struggles with their child. There was one mom who would not take her eyes off her baby. She stood by the baby's side watching for hours and hours with no break. I watched another mom almost ignore her child's cries and seem to be numb. I watched some infants whose parents hardly ever visited because it was just too hard for the parent to be there.

I held my son's hand for over 10 hours one night. I couldn't leave his side. He wouldn't let go. My hand was going numb, but I didn't care. It felt like I had unending energy to give. But by the second round of hospitalizations, I was more exhausted. I had been through this before and I had little to no recovery time in between.

During my second experience at the ICU, there were times when I found myself feeling annoyed by the needs and crying of the other children in the ICU. It was stressful. Again, I sat in judgment of myself. I'm a compassionate, caring person who cannot stand to see anyone suffer, yet here I was, annoyed by the crying of very sick children. I hoped my child would sleep and not need me to hold his hand all night, and I felt selfish. Again, compassion fatigue was at work and would show up in my life again and again.

So how can you avoid compassion fatigue and/or treat it if it shows up in your life? First, as you have heard me say, don't judge yourself. Again, there are no right or wrong ways to approach the circumstances of your life. You are finding yourself and your child in new and extreme situations. Judging yourself does not do anyone any good. It only serves to further stress and fatigue you. You may judge yourself anyway. We tend to do that when under stress. When there is a crisis or something goes very wrong in life, we tend to blame ourselves or look for someone else to blame. It's just part of the human condition and it's not your fault.

You might even find yourself "judge the judging," as Tara Brach, a psychologist, author, and Buddhist teacher, discusses in her work. I had an occasion to talk with Tara Brach when I attended a retreat she led two summers ago. I talked with her about my experiences with my son. She told me, "You were in crisis and it makes sense you judged yourself and judged yourself for judging." I thanked her for her words of wisdom and validation. I share them here now in hopes that it somehow helps you as well. Be kind to yourself in your thoughts. Compassion fatigue sets in when we forget to feel compassion for ourselves.

You can also avoid compassion fatigue and caregiver stress by delegating as much as possible. Allow others to step in if possible. "Putting on the brake so you don't break" is something I tell my patients, and it's a good way to look at it.

I didn't do a great job of delegating. In fact, I remember feeling that I could not step away from my son. There was actually so much going on every moment that it seemed physically impossible to leave his side. The hospital only allowed one parent to stay in the room, so my husband was often at the hotel. I was it.

One very rough night, my son asked that my husband not leave the hospital. He gave me a break when he could, and slept on the window sill of the family waiting room. I would wait until he got into the room to leave my son's side, even just to use the bathroom. I remember racing through a shower, not allowing myself to feel restored by the water, so I could get back to my son.

Did it really need to be like that? There I was in the shower with nothing I could do at that moment but feel the water on my skin, but I wasn't even aware of it. Instead, I found myself worrying and picturing the worst outcomes. I was also judging myself, blaming myself somehow. Was I just going to stay on the horrible ride and keep feeling awful and getting lost in worry and being a terrible mom? That was certainly not helping anyone.

During my son's second round of surgeries, I tried to do it differently. This time I was able to step away and also use those moments to refuel a bit. I took a shower and focused only on the water washing over my body. I imagined a calm forest with a gentle stream and surrounded myself with light and love from the universe. I soaked that all in.

I also was able to sit by my son's side and focus on that same light and energy. I imagined and connected to a light all around us. I relied more heavily on the sense of energy, support from the universe. I prayed by asking for light, love, and energy from the universe and from my deceased parents and grandparents that had died many years before. I asked the universe to support me. I saw myself supported.

I felt more cared for and less fatigued despite the longer hours of each of the surgeries. I felt less drained – even though things were even more stressful because the tumor had returned and this was the second time we were going through all of this. I was amazed at the differences in how I felt.

One major thing I did differently was to use my imagery and thoughts to take breaks and support myself. I responded to my feelings and thoughts with much less judgment. There was no energy to waste blaming myself, judging myself, and reacting to images. I let things go. I allowed the flow.

Focusing on what was right and on gratitude also helped me handle the compassion fatigue. In addition to delegating where possible, it's very useful to think about what is going well. It may be challenging, but something is always going right. If you are breathing, then something is right. You can be grateful for even the smallest things, even a glass of water. It helps when compassion fatigue sets in.

CHAPTER 3

Maintaining Psychological and Physical Wellness

"Your beliefs and thoughts are wired into your biology."
-Dr. Christiane Northrup

During one of my son's hospital stays, I noticed a mom who had been dealing with her child's illness for quite a while. She was sitting in the doctor's waiting room for an extended time. She was offered water, tea, or some beverage and snack. Her decline almost seemed reflexive. "I'm fine," she said. "I don't need anything. My child is sick, but I'm fine."

I knew she was likely hungry and thirsty. She may have not been aware of it, or if she was, she was kind of deciding to go without. We do that. It's part of the crisis and circumstances. I certainly did that, and at times, still do. But I see more clearly now that there is a choice to take the opportunity to care for oneself. I see how the neglect of self can lead to a bigger crisis and add to the long-term trauma and compromise to health.

How can you possibly take care of yourself when your child is dealing with such a serious medical issue? How can you possibly remain psychologically and physically well and balanced? It seems impossible, and yet, it's critical. Because the adrenaline that is so ever-present in crisis can only take you so far. It may last for a long while depending on your health and age, but at some point, your body will let you know that it can't carry on – even when your brain is telling you that you must.

I know a dad who suffered from stomach problems due to the stress of his child's medical issues. He already had some health issues, and the stress exacerbated his symptoms. He had also stopped eating well, saying that "there is no time and I'll deal with that later." He said he had to focus on his child. Months later, he found himself in the ER with his own health crisis. He had ignored symptoms and was in excruciating pain. He was forced to pay attention to his body.

Steps for Wellness

Simple steps for wellness are possible even at the most difficult of times. Anything you do or have done that promotes wellness is valuable. The list in Appendix I provides some examples of ways you can support physical and psychological health.

Some examples include:

- Health-promoting vitamins, supplements and formulas, Rescue Remedy and adrenal support formulas.
- Stress-reducing foods.
- Water, water, water.
- Regardless of what you eat, eat a bit slower if you can. Allow your food to slowly digest as you take it in. This can have a tremendous effect on reducing stomach upset even if you're eating unhealthy foods.
- L.I.F.E. breathing: Practice being in your body. Notice the feel of the chair you're sitting on. Practice letting go and living in the moments of your day. Practice positive imagery/meditation exercises such as the one below.

Meditation: Visualize Health, Energy, and Wellness

Imagine for a moment that you can see yourself in a calm and relaxing place. Take a few deep breaths and bring that calm into all the cells of your body. Imagine there is a place to walk, swim, or exercise as you prefer. Imagine, for example, taking a nice hike in a wooded forest or along a quiet beach. You can see the waves, perhaps, and hear the way they wash up onto the shore. You can feel the breeze. You can change this to something you like in any way you want. See yourself enjoying the walk and imagine you are feeling well and balanced. Imagine you can place your worries down for a moment in a safe place, in a container or box of some sort, and come back for them in a little while. Imagine the lightness in your walk now. You can walk, run, swim, or engage in any activity that feels like a fit for you now. You can also just sit and stretch out, or even float on a cloud. Whatever you imagine is perfect for you and will help you now.

Enjoy this space. Feel the health and wellness soaking into every part of you. You are strong, rested, and well. Look around and see if there is anything you would like to take with you from this wonderful place. You can take that with you now – perhaps a small stone or symbol or even a message that you can carry with you always. Take that with you now as you begin to head back.

Stepping back now toward the container where you left your worries and concerns, you open the container and see these items. Perhaps you may want to leave some of them there. You can always come back and get them. They are safe there and you are safe and well. You can continue along your path now as you make your way back to the present time. As you come back into your space in the room, you can feel your body in the chair. Feel the peace and wellness in your entire body. Make your way back into your space feeling energized and well.

As the father who landed in the ER learned, taking care of your body is incredibly important – but that's easy to lose perspective on when your life changes in the blink of an eye during your child's medical crisis.

I remember watching a parent getting a massage while in the pediatric ICU. I think it was hospital-coordinated somehow. I recall thinking I really needed that massage, too. My back was in so much pain from sleeping on the "parent chair/bed." But I was so worn out and in such a crisis mindset that I didn't even have the energy to inquire.

I had a patient, a parent whose child was ill, share with me that she hadn't slept for days on end. She said she wasn't even fatigued. The adrenaline that was pouring into her bloodstream from the crisis of her child's medical issue kept her going. She could not recall when she had eaten and wasn't sure whether her last meal had been a sandwich provided by the hospital or if she had ordered food. Another parent said "Food? What food? I have no appetite. My kid is trying to stay alive. I don't really care about eating."

One parent joked that he didn't understand why the hospital provided a parent locker with shower facilities. There were no towels and he didn't have time to shower or really care if he showered. "Who cares if I stink," he said. "That's the last thing on my mind."

Probably people have told you to "please take care of you so you can take care of your child," but while this is absolutely true, those words can seem empty and meaningless when you are in crisis. Particularly as a parent, you may find the norm of sacrifice for your child to be ever-present. You may even have had a moment when you actually are aware you are sacrificing and suffering because your child is suffering, and you feel that's appropriate: "I'm going to go without because we are in crisis."

Perhaps you may experience another type of response to the stress of your child's medical issue. Maybe you are in fact focused on your own needs to the point of detaching from your child's suffering. Sometimes we need distance and to avoid the entire ordeal by a sort of distraction. "I'm going to go eat out and stay out of that hospital," one parent told me. "They don't need me here and I'm probably just in the way." Please don't judge yourself for any of these experiences. It's all normal. It's all part of your experience. It's part of coping.

Mary, a mom with a child with a chronic serious illness, remembered having a pedicure and realizing she wasn't even in her body and aware of having a foot massage because she was so lost in her thoughts. She said she wanted to go back for a second pedicure and actually be at the appointment instead of lost in thought and planning, panicking, and worrying. She said she had a break and yet she forgot to take it. Such important words!

We absolutely should and can take the breaks that we have when we have them. Honor and embrace those moments. Like Mary having her pedicure, use the moments to connect with and support yourself in the present.

Nick has a son with leukemia. He has a break and goes to golf with his friends. But the entire time, he is thinking about his son and not able to enjoy his golf break. John has a daughter with a brain tumor. He goes to the gym and feels guilty for not being with his daughter every moment.

Again, this is normal and not to ever be judged. Things are hard enough without you criticizing yourself. You truly are doing the best you can. Your brain is naturally going to be in almost constant problem-solving mode. You are in crisis. But you can try to be present in your body and be in the moment. Realizing you have been lost in thought is actually a waking up of sorts. You now have awareness that you were not aware. That is the moment to then be connected to the moments and your body.

Even in small ways, if you can care for your own health and wellness, it helps you have the energy to face the unique issues that can occur particularly as you encounter the medical settings and medical situations with your child.

Practice

Take a moment to breathe and connect to your present moments right now. Feel your body in the chair or space you are in. If you notice any tension, see if you can let that go. Notice the space around you. Any thoughts and worries are perfectly ok to notice, too.

CHAPTER 4

Managing Medical Settings and Situations

"Life doesn't get easier or more forgiving. We get stronger and more resilient."

-Dr. Steven Maraboli

One parent said that one of her worst moments was when she had to hold her child down for a painful medical procedure. You want to protect your child, and your instinct is to want to scoop them up and take them away. Instead, you have to allow procedures that are painful and upsetting to your child. You may have to allow toxic medicines to be poured into your child's body that are supposed to help, and yet you know your child will be very sick from those medicines. Witnessing your child's struggles is one of the most challenging aspects of parenting.

Take a moment right now and take a deep breath. You may want to practice the L.I.F.E breathing technique. This is helpful particularly as you focus on the issues related to medical settings and situations. The medical stuff is the hardest. It's where the trauma is happening or happened. Perhaps even imagine that protective energizing light around you and your family. This light can be used at any time. Even in the most difficult moments in the most challenging environments, you can tap into that protective, energizing light.

I can't know what your particular circumstances are in your life and what that is like for you. I find that even two parents with the exact same circumstances will experience it differently. I do know that the circumstances are unbelievable at times. It's terrible that your child is so seriously at risk or sick and that their life is filled with medical appointments, scans, hospitals, and/or surgeries. It's heartbreaking that you have to watch your child in medical situations that many adults never even have to experience. It's surreal what is going on.

The list of new experiences is unique and can include:

- Hearing your child has a serious or life-threatening medical issue.
- Going for medical tests and scans with your child.
- Waiting and waiting for results of scans and medical tests
- Waiting in doctors' offices, surgical waiting rooms, and treatment facilities.
- Holding your child while treatments and medical tests and procedures occur.

What can help? One tip I learned to help manage some of the medical information is to keep a notebook and a file with all necessary information. I found that writing down as much information as possible helped with specific details and minimized overwhelm from having no notes or notes in multiple places. I found a binder or notebook with sections to be useful. You can make the sections whatever works for you. I had a medical information section. I had a running list of things to do section. I had an ongoing notes from phone calls section. I had a section right in the front with important phone numbers, fax numbers, email addresses, and addresses for doctors. I later added a section of supportive resources and helpful things to do for myself. I also added positive images, pictures, and imagery exercises for support.

Even with a binder for support, there are things that come up for which you can't and won't be prepared. I recall walking out of the hospital room while the doctors removed some packing from my son's nose after his first surgery. I had not realized the doctors were going to start the procedure, and I answered my phone thinking I had a moment. The doctors had previously told me it was going to be rough and they would administer pain meds ahead of time.

I had not left my son's side for more than a moment during that hospital stay, but ironically, it turned out that I was out of the room for most of the packing removal procedure. There was a team of surgeons and residents around my son's bed and no room for me. I had planned to stay off to the side, but by the time I returned, the procedure was almost complete.

I initially felt guilty I hadn't been in the room. How could I step away when my son was in so much pain and so afraid? I had sat with him through everything I could. I held his hand through scan after scan. I would have even stayed in the operating room if they had let me. But that moment of guilt later turned into recognition that I could let go. I started to see how strong my son was and how brave of a young man he actually was. I also saw the strength in myself at being able to let go.

One mom, Kathy, told me about her son's ongoing struggles with illness during one of her psychotherapy session meetings with me. She said she felt so vulnerable and upset, continually seeing her son in such pain. She felt helpless and hopeless. She saw him struggle and witnessed her own emotional pain, fear, and agony. She wished she could trade places with him. She saw how brave he was and thought herself "weak" for not being able to be as brave.

I listened to her describe the circumstances and how she put herself down for not behaving "stronger" in front of her son and others. I heard her guilt and self-judgment. I asked her what part of her was brave. She did not see any at the moment. I asked her how she thought her son saw her. She paused, but then started to see herself through her son's eyes. She started to see her bravery as she described taking her son for appointments and treatments and always being by his side. Yes, she was vulnerable and felt "weak," but she was also strong. She was forgetting to embrace that part of herself.

So while there are no clear or easy solutions to the challenges inherent in the medical situations and settings that you have and perhaps still will face, the helpful news is that there are some choices as to how you go through those situations.

Humor

Use of humor wherever possible can help. Parents inflating the rubber gloves and playing a game is a common example. I remember laughing at my son pretending to be E.T. with his finger monitor that lit up red in the dark room. "E.T. phone home," he said. I didn't even realize he was familiar with the movie. It was hilarious and we laughed.

Go "Two" People

It's helpful to have a person or two that are your main supports. These are the go "two" people. These are people who can listen the way you need them to listen, get tasks done for you, and be a general source of strength. It may surprise you who these people turn out to be. They may not be the best friends or family members that you have thought of as the people you turn to in times of challenge. These may be people you know but are not in your immediate circle of contacts. It may be surprising who will help once they know you are in need. Your immediate family may be, understandably, too upset and traumatized.

That's normal and fine by the way, but you can make decisions to draw lines around how much you listen to others' worries. There is nothing helpful about hearing about everyone else's stress response at times. I recall a friend saying to me, "So you're just supposed to wait for these tumors to come back? How can you live that way?"

So finding useful and helpful support is absolutely going to be a benefit. Sometimes people will ask what they can do and you may be able to give them a specific answer. These may be people that are not in your immediate circle of contacts and yet, somehow, your paths cross and there is an opportunity to ask and even accept an offer of help. Take that offer and opportunity if you can even if it seems odd that it is coming from a person who was not so close prior to your child's medical issue.

If you do get some unhelpful responses and offers, you can choose not to accept and take those in. It is an understandable response, but not helpful to hear comments such as other people's worries or even their ideas about what things are like for you for example, I chose to not take comments like that in at those moments. This is an example of hearing without attaching to things that happen or what people say. It can give you a choice and some sense of control at times that seem out of control. If you can choose your response to something, then you actually have quite a bit of freedom. Being able to say to yourself something like "those words are not helpful to me right now and more about that person. While they may have good intentions, that is not helpful to me and so I'm not going to take those words in. Instead I will move on to more helpful words and ideas."

Practical Tips for Going to the Hospital

One parent told me she was packing for a hospital stay and suddenly realized it was like getting ready for an unplanned vacation – except, of course, this was not going to be a vacation. It had not occurred to her that leaving her home for her daughter's surgery would entail placing her dog in a kennel, making hotel reservations, and making arrangements for her mail and other household maintenance. She was going to need to arrange for her other children's care as well. She had to pack a bag for herself and was unsure what to bring. She asked what would help to have handy.

What to pack may seem like the least of the issues you face, but its importance will become clear once you're at the hospital. When I packed for my first hospital stay with my son, I brought way too much. I really just needed yoga pants and sweatshirts along with my toiletries and small electronics. The second time I was with my son for his hospital stay, I brought much less and added a yoga mat to put on a portable cot that folded up into a backpack-type carrier. I had a real problem sleeping on the parent bed/chair that was provided. I had huge trouble and complications with my back. It was a bit of joke at the ICU of the hospital that only a parent with some experience would think to bring her own bed and yoga mat.

Some things to pack:

- comfortable clothing such as sweatpants and yoga pants
- small electronics with headphones
- healthy, non-perishable snacks
- minimal but necessary toiletries
- yoga mat and small pillow
- a small favorite item for your child such as a well-loved game, toy, or pillow

Surviving Some of the Worst Moments

Like the mom who struggled with having to hold her child down, every parent has their own version of the worst moments. You can take a moment now and ask yourself, "What are the worst things I've experienced with my child?" What was the worst of the worst? How did you get through those moments?

One of the hardest moments for me was the fear that my child would not make it through surgery. I imagined the surgeon coming out to tell me that my son did not survive. I had mostly not allowed myself to think that way. I knew it was possible, but I did not focus on it consciously at all. But on the last day of his second surgery, it hit me like a huge tsunami moment. It was not a thought, really, it was more like a movie playing before my very eyes. I could see it happening. It took my breath away. I imagined getting through a funeral. Incredible and awful. I did not know how I would go on, but I knew somehow I would. I don't know how, but somehow I got up and walked around. I started to deep breathe. Walking around and breathing helped.

During your worst moments, remember to practice L.I.F.E. breathing, connecting to positive energy, and calling upon your spiritual beliefs, whatever they may be, to stay present. It may feel like the last thing you want to do, to stay present in that horrible moment, but staying present is absolutely what will get you through.

Managing the medical stuff in any way you can is the right way for you. Even if you never remember to do anything I've mentioned, you can survive and manage. Your body and your instinct will know what to do. We are hardwired for survival. The strategies I mention will serve to add to your resources. This helps particularly as you face other areas of changes in your child, family, and social support systems.

CHAPTER 5

Changing Social Connections

---

*"I see my child changing. I see my whole world changing.
Everything is different and everyone seems different."*
-Me, 2014

Just at a time when you need your friends for support, they may not know how to help. They may not know what to say. They may drop out of sight.

As for those who do speak up, their well-intentioned comments might not help, and may even make things worse: "Everything will be fine," "God doesn't give you more than you can handle," "This is a blessing in disguise," "It's really not that bad," "I know someone who has a child that is sick," and the well-meaning but ultimately empty, "Let me know if you need help."

Many parents have told me that they felt completely exasperated and in need of support, but at the same time, felt totally isolated. One parent said that she felt like they were now "that family that everyone knows who has a sick kid. Everyone just looks at us differently. Many people say nothing to me and even avoid me. Are you kidding me? They can't catch what my kid has!"

When there is a serious or life-threatening medical issue in the family, the health crisis is often and understandably the focus of conversation. It's what is going on. Particularly if it was a sudden change, it will dominate almost every aspect of your existence and be part of the first questions you are asked. While that is normal and helpful, it can also negate the rest of life's experiences. One parent exclaimed, "My child is more than this disease!"

It can be supportive and validating to have friends and others ask how your family is doing, how your child is doing, and how you are managing as a parent. It acknowledges and validates what is currently happening. It gives you the opportunity to share. Having a friend or someone who can truly listen is one of the best gifts. Sometimes, however, people are not able to actually listen to your experience and provide space in conversation for your need to talk. Some people are afraid to discuss terrifying topics when a child's life is at risk. Or they don't know what to say, so they avoid the topic or even avoid contact entirely. Others may feel they want to help, solve problems, and look for encouraging news. "At least you are _____," that kind of comment. This can shift the focus of the conversation to their agenda rather than creating space for you. This is challenging, particularly when things may not be going well or if your child is terminal.

The important thing is to remember that whatever the response from others, it says more about their experience and likely has nothing to do with you. It is also very crucial to remember that while someone choosing to avoid contact may hurt and can be very difficult for you, it is not personal. Most people don't know how to respond to huge challenges. In fact, our society, in general, doesn't embrace how to be fully present, particularly with big events and devastating circumstances. It's nobody's fault, but it is good to be aware that it may happen before you actually encounter it.

One key strategy to cope with this change in social contact is to recognize and allow this without focusing and getting stuck on what is not working. I often tell my patients to allow it to be what it is – even get upset about it – but at some point, move on to what is working. Find a person that can simply listen to whatever you have to say or be present with whatever you don't want to say. I often felt that I couldn't stop talking about it sometimes, and at other times, I couldn't talk about it at all. Again, you are in charge and you get to choose what fits for you. This is part of you creating and maintaining your own personal lifeline. If you can't seem to find any person at a time you need to express your thoughts and feelings, you can write, you can blog or post, you can call a professional. You can also go to the LIFELINE Facebook page (@Parentsofchildrenwithlifethreateningmedicalissue), or e-mail me directly at: Drmorett@valstar.net

You may be dismayed by the people who don't show up for you, but you will likely also be surprised by the ones who do. We can have connections and support from new places and people just when we least expect it. Crisis and challenges open us at times. That stranger at the grocery store that says something perfectly supportive at just the right moment can be everything you needed at that moment. The admiration from another parent in the doctor's office can be a real connection. Finding a support network that suddenly opens you up to all kinds of new people can make all the difference in your life.

I'll never forget the times of feeling complete exasperation with and disconnection from the rest of the world. I was so worn out and feeling alone and a sense of total collapse seemed near. I felt alone and thought that nobody seemed to understand what I was experiencing. I lost the energy to reach out. I shut down. Many of the parents I have treated describe this kind of isolation: shut down and shut off from others.

For me, there were well-meaning friends and family that tried to say supportive words. Some people even tried to tell me that it wasn't as bad as I thought it was and that I was exaggerating! That really enraged me and led to further isolation and loneliness. "They don't get me," I told myself, which only led to more anger, hurt, and continued isolation. I know I focused on these feelings too often and for far too long. If there is one thing I can look back on and see now, it's that I used up precious energy being hurt and angry. I wished I'd spent a little less time on all that, acknowledging it only to a degree and then moving on to a better focus and more helpful perspective.

Friends may encourage you to attend social gatherings. Some may even get upset that you've stopped communicating. It's possible you feel, as I did, that people in general do not understand how your life has changed and how your social life and need for contact have also changed. Some of your friends may feel like total strangers. I remember one friend who was likely scared for me saying, "You just felt like it was that bad, but I'm sure it was not that bad." That was a conversation ender. Not helpful, and it left me with no energy to do anything but get off the phone.

But sometimes, that seeming lack of support is your story, not what's true. One day, I called the school attendance office for what seemed like the umpteenth time to report that my child was going to be out sick. I almost felt embarrassed that once again he was not going to school. It's crazy, but the denial like my friend's, above, of the severity of the circumstances and the risk to my child's life had me doubting myself at times. I began judging: "Why is he missing all this school when he's not really sick? The school is starting to think we are being educationally neglectful."

The attendance staff member on the call, who I had never met, offered words of encouragement. "He needs to rest. It's just school. It's so hard on you all," she offered. It was the first time I felt that someone from outside actually understood. I had spoken with this attendance person countless times and had never met her, yet she felt like a friend every time I called and would continue to need to call over the course of two years. She always offered kind and supportive words. For that I was grateful. It is a precious example of a stranger that nonetheless was a tremendous friend and was part of my own personal lifeline when I felt I had nothing to hold onto.

Friends show up in both expected and unexpected places. One of my son's first nurses, Kate, showed up at the exact moment she was needed. She saved us both. After a very long surgery with lots of complications, there was Kate in the pediatric ICU. She had an energy and way of connecting with my son that was miraculous. She spoke with him with such kindness, support, and playfulness. She was there for most of the worst moments. She was there. She was just there. She did her nursing to care for him, but just as important, she was able to be with us all. She became a family friend. She was encouraging without being ridiculously upbeat. We keep in touch still.

It's extremely challenging when you as the parent feel alone and unsupported, and it makes it harder to support and assist your child. Take a look at Appendix II for some ideas of how to both hold boundaries and ask for meaningful help. Establishing a support resource for yourself is part of adding to your own personal lifeline.

CHAPTER 6

Changes in the Child

"It is during our darkest moments that we must focus to see the light."

-Aristotle Onassis

How You and Others View Your Child

Changes in appearance and size are a normal part of your child's development, and you and others are used to that. But now, maybe the way they look is changing in a different way. This might happen quickly, as with hair loss due to medical treatments, or body-altering surgery. It might happen more gradually, as your child's energy and stamina fluctuate. Sometimes a child's outward appearance does not change at all. This can also complicate responses from others in conversation, as people may not understand or may minimize the medical issue.

Even you might struggle with the changes in your child's appearance or personality. You may see pain, struggle, and suffering in place of what was carefree joy or energy driven toward some interest, goal, or direction. Now it feels as if that is all gone. Now it may feel like your child's life has completely changed. It has. You don't know where your child is headed and what life will hold.

This is where focusing on your child's qualities of *being* beyond the things they are able to *do* is key. Now, more than ever, there's an opportunity for you to see your child in a different way as they develop through their struggles. You would never, ever say it's a good thing, but since it's happening, it's important to see what is coming to you and your child through these experiences. It's also different than that extremely unhelpful "blessing in disguise" type of comment.

This is more of a moment of seeing life and the universe from bigger perspective. Really big here, really big. The kind of perspective that has deeper meaning. Your child is being called upon to deal with incredible challenges and their bravery is showing through. Your child is a sweet soul and so much more than how she looks, her grades, or what she does.

My mentor, Beth Darlington, told me in a recent meeting that my son was on a hero's journey. She was referring to the classic journey, as told by writers from Homer to Joseph Campbell, where the hero goes to hell and back. He returns changed forever. He brings gifts to the world and it changes his life and the world around him in powerful ways.

I did not get upset when Beth spoke those words. I did not see it as a statement that my child was fortunate in any way and that it was good his life was at risk. I had to be ready for that bigger view, and I would not tell you that it is easy or the first line of coping. I would not jump right in right away and lead with "Oh, your child is a hero," as it can sound dismissive of the struggle. It is, however, there on some level for the taking if you want to see it. I share these words here with you not to say there is anything good about your child's medical struggle, but it is happening. You did not choose it, but you can choose how you see it. You can see the power of it.

It can be very empowering to see your child as a hero. That's the kind of BIG perspective that can make a big difference.

How Your Child Views Themselves

Often, children with medical issues want to be "normal" – particularly if their medical issue was sudden and not a condition at birth. Your child wants to have their normal life back. They want to do what they have always done. They don't want to be "special" and stand out in a group. Yet, they do on some level appreciate and enjoy some of the attention. We all do.

Your child may identify with the "sick" role, and this has subtle and not-so-subtle effects on their experiences as well as yours. Their ability to acknowledge their medical issue can validate their reality and help them cope. But it can be hard on you. It can be devastating and heartbreaking for you to witness your child identifying themselves completely with the medical issue and losing touch with the other parts of their life and experience. The subtleties of this "sick" identity can include a sense of helplessness at times for your child.

One of my patients shared that she noticed her child just assuming there was no point to try to do some school work or organize her room. Her daughter told her she was "sick and I can't do anything anymore." While it was certainly true that her daughter was not well at all, there were times she had more energy and was feeling well, as indicated one day by her laughing, playing, and jumping around. When her mom asked her to help set the table, the child sat down and claimed she was "sick."

What the child was doing in that moment was identifying with the "sick" role. She wasn't manipulating, she actually felt like it was her role not to be capable of helping with family tasks because at times that was the case. She actually assumed she was "too sick" to help. I recommended that she talk to her daughter and help her recall the examples of when she felt strong. We spoke about her child being a warrior princess and then dressing up to dance around the house. They were able to put on music and use those ideas to help her child connect to an empowered image and feeling.

Social Changes for Your Child

Most likely, your child's activities and school performance have changed. This can also extend to social changes. Children connect through their school, extracurricular activities, and attendance at events. Your child may not be able to go to school or attend athletic events, parties, field trips, etc.

One thing you and your child may experience is others not inviting your child to visit their home or to participate in events or outings. People may be unsure if your child is well enough to attend a social event. I fully believe that some people don't want to have a child with a serious medical situation in their care. Perhaps they are afraid something will happen or that they will need to make some accommodations that will ruin the social event. Perhaps they are concerned the social event will be somehow negatively affected by the child's presence. People often withdraw as a way to deal. I hear many stories of families reporting that others thought it best not to bother them. People may feel they are being kind and respectful by giving you and your family space. There may actually be very good intentions here. People are busy, and they may also make assumptions about your child and family.

Whatever the reason, it can be frustrating, painful, and angering to feel that your child and your family are being excluded – especially at a time when you really need connection. It's completely understandable to experience such feelings. It's also normal and common for you to feel too tired, not have time, or to not feel able to make the effort to reach out to others.

Feeling alone and scared yourself while also having to help your child with feeling alone and scared, can be extremely challenging. Your child "shouldn't have to deal with all these social changes" while also battling a life-threatening medical issue. As one of my patients said, "Isn't it enough that he has to go through all this? Now his friends have stopped calling.

Now I'm watching my child become so upset when he misses out on parties he comes to discover already happened."

Solutions

Breathe and practice L.I.F.E breathing. Your experience is completely normal and valid no matter what's going on, and that awareness can be empowering. Utilize the lifeline you're creating for your support. Experience feeling very angry and infuriated. At some point, perhaps, you'll let it go. I'm sure you don't want to waste precious energy and brain power running this through your mind over and over. It can hijack your energy and precious time.

Also, be open to surprising social connections. We may not know how it will come about, but often the right thing shows up at the right moment. Your child may even find a connection with other children with medical issues (some children may resist this option as they don't want to be seen and identified with the "sick" group of children). You never know what is possible.

School-aged children – and particularly middle and high school-aged children – will experience this on a different level. Peer groups and friendships often change during the teen years. Teens tend to want to spend time away from the family and establish their separate identity. An older child with a medical issue may have complications related to this transition in development. They may want to be separate and independent, and yet have medical issues may make that challenging.

Technology can actually be a helpful resource as a way to address connections and changes in a child's social life. Having the ability to be on social media, play video games online together, text friends, and call on Skype can be helpful resource to stay connected. I know many families that have chronicled their experiences with pictures and videos. I know of one teen that recorded much of his experience with his medical issues so that he could share with others.

CHAPTER 7

Changes in the Family

"Do what you can, with what you have, where you are."
-Theodore Roosevelt

The level of stress of your child's medical issue is not a surprise given the unbelievable challenges. The effects are not limited, as you likely already know, to just your child and the medical issue, but in fact have far-reaching extended effects on the world around you. This of course includes your family. The level of added stress affects everyone in the family. Having an awareness of this fact can help when extra challenges pop up.

Parents may become less patient with one another. Some parents begin to fight as they take the stress out on one another. And some couples actually find they are increasingly bonded as a result of the challenges. Single parents, divorced parents, stepparents, there are as many circumstances and unique reactions/responses as there are families.

All the thoughts and feelings that come along with a serious medical issue most certainly have an effect on the relationship between you and your child as well, beginning with how to explain what is happening and finding that line between honesty and being overwhelming or scary.

At one point, my son looked me in the eye and asked if he was going to die. This is one of those "worst moments." I responded with empathy – "That must be so scary, to be worried about that" – and with positivity: "I'm right here with you, and everyone is doing everything they can to take care of you." How to respond to your child's questions and how much to explain depends on your child's age, diagnosis, prognosis, and many other unique and individual circumstances. It's too complicated for one, simple, universal answer. Children need the honest truth when the truth is definitive and not going to change, as with a terminal diagnosis. But when outcomes are uncertain, the best thing you can do is be honest with the uncertainty, to acknowledge their fear and worry, and to emphasize what you and your child's medical team are doing to help.

Sibling relationships change, too. Your child's brothers and/or sisters are understandably upset, but they show their feelings and reactions in their own unique ways. Some siblings become caretakers, some may act out to get attention, and some may be jealous and actually say they wish they were "sick" so they could get everyone's attention.

It's not unlike when a new baby comes into the house and everyone forgets about the older sibling – except this is a crisis and not celebratory attention. Still, the siblings of a child with a medical issue may in fact act like they are jealous. They may be feeling a sense of neglect and that the attention they receive from you is less than it was before. Your availability and attention are most certainly compromised, which makes perfect sense. You are in crisis. Siblings may act out, as children often do, in response to the added stress. That acting out adds to the stress level in the family and presents even greater challenges for you as the parent.

Siblings can also become "parentified" and start to take on caretaker roles. I know parents who have described even very young siblings that will start to cook, clean, or try to help out in any way possible. I've known siblings to become very active in caring for their sibling with a medical issue. Of course on some level this can be helpful, but it can also have a negative effect on the sibling, due to them stalling on or sacrificing their own needs.

There is no single easy answer to address this dynamic and it certainly varies from family to family, but it can help to let your other children know that you value them and see them just for who they are being and appreciate their help, too. It also helps to try to talk about and focus on other topics beyond the challenges and the medical issue. If possible, try to spend time alone with your other children – even just a moment sometimes may help. Making sure you give some attention to your other children, even just to say you like their hair or the way they smile. It can make a big difference.

Your relationship with yourself and just about everyone in your life will be different, and that's understandable. You can decide how much you want to be in contact with others. If it is not helpful, you can refrain from contact in order to support yourself. When feeling particularly overwhelmed, it can be worse to be in contact with others, especially if they are expressing their anxiety and stress response.

It may also help to practice connecting to a positive, supportive "other" through an imagery exercise – particularly if there is not a person available in your life or at the time you need that person. Imagining a supportive presence can actually help. It may sound a bit odd, but it works.

Practice: Imagining a Supportive Relationship

Take a moment and breathe. Practice L.I.F.E. breathing for a few moments. See if you can feel your body and notice any places of tension and let them go just a bit. Keep breathing in a natural way. Picture a pleasing image. Anything will work and is fine for you. Enjoy those images even if your mind gets distracted and you have worries. The positive, pleasing images are there, too. Enjoy that place for a bit. Now, try thinking of a person or some wise being that you admire. This being can be a real person, a spiritual figure or being, or anyone that comes to mind. Focus on that being. Practice having that being right here with you now. This being is wise, loving, strong, supportive, and knows exactly what you need. Breathe in that support and love into all the cells of your body. That energy is empowering and supportive and with you at all times. You are loved and protected. You can trust that energy. You have that energy now and with you at all times. Really bring that energy and being with you into your life. After a while, you can focus on the feel of your body in your space. You are feeling empowered and a sense of strength. If you want, you can write about the being that you imagined and the benefits that being provides.

CHAPTER 8

Transformation Beyond Trauma

"I never met a strong person with an easy past."

-Anonymous

"When is the next horrible thing going to happen to my child?" one dad asked. He had reached the point where he noticed no difference between crisis anxiety and every day stress. Everything constantly felt like the bottom would drop out again at any moment. He described "flashbacks" of the day his child was diagnosed, the treatments, the worry, and countless upsetting images. Like a movie constantly playing and flashing in his head, on and on and on. How do we change that and stop this repetitive swirling?

Is it possible for you to heal and feel less traumatized after going through or still living with such serious medical issues present for your child? It may seem impossible, like those images are seared into your brain. Your body and mindset now function differently as a result. It likely is not something you feel you have control over and you may think you will be this way permanently.

It is amazingly true, however, that you can shift your experience and heal from trauma even when it is ongoing. I've developed some steps to do just that, and you can try them any time. I'll outline them, and then you can practice them anytime that feels right.

First, it is very important, when you are ready, to tell your story and all the feelings, thoughts, and experiences. You can talk about it to someone who can just listen, write about it even if nobody ever reads it, blog about it, or even meet with a professional where a safe space can be created for you to express and be with your experiences.

If you're truly ready, it is important that you share whatever you want and hold nothing back. Nothing, absolutely nothing. You are in control here. There isn't anything too awful to say or write. It's something you may need to do many times. There are new experiences, new memories, and new pieces to share. You do not have to share it all at once – and only do this if it feels like a fit at the time.

The most important point here is if you do NOT feel ready, then you need to trust yourself on that and recall what I've said before, that there are no rules and no right or wrong ways to be. So, if it feels best right now to not think about or express your experiences yet, please trust that and absolutely do not share, write or speak until you feel ready. Not sharing is actually a terrific option. I call it healthy avoidance. It's crucial that we can choose to not connect with our thoughts and feelings when it feels like it is the wrong time.

If you feel you may be ready, you can test this out and give it a try. Consider pausing for a moment after you read the next few sentences. Think about an image or a thought about your experiences with your child. Now, ask yourself: do I want to share this with someone? Do I feel ready to spend some time thinking and feeling about this? Do I want to write about it even if it won't be read by anyone? Really sit with those questions and trust that your inner wise self will know the perfect answer for you. Keep checking with that inner part of you. It really does know best.

If you get the go ahead and it feels right to share your story, then do it in any way that feels right for you. If you are going to share it verbally with someone, make sure that person knows their job is to only listen without commenting. If you're writing and others will read it, the same thing applies. You do not have to read any responses from others. You also do not have to post the writing or share it in any way. The expression of your story is more important than anything on the receiving end. Just telling your story in any form that makes sense for you is the first step.

And here is another critical part of this step: please never judge a thing! Everything you feel, think, and experience is perfectly perfect for you. It's all fine to be there and you do not have to react to it at all. That mindfulness piece is so important. You can notice and observe what you are feeling, thinking, and experiencing while it is happening. That will actually help you feel even more empowered.

One example that comes up frequently is anger. You may feel some intense anger about something – especially about your child having a medical issue. It may seem overwhelming, but it's okay to be angry. It's okay when you're expressing your story to get angry and express that, too. Noticing it is very different than any actions you may take about it. Noticing without judgment is mindfulness, and it creates healing and empowerment.

A second important step is to get validation for your experiences. Once you have shared your story, it's crucial to get the message that it is all okay. You can give yourself that now, as you're reading what I'm saying. Everything you feel, think, and experience is valid and okay – even if you believe you are the only one to ever have those thoughts, feelings, and experiences. This may come up for you particularly if your child has a rare medical issue or if you have not connected with anyone that has had similar experiences. It's all okay. It's not that you feel okay and things will work out okay, but more that no matter what your experience, it is absolutely 100% valid. Nothing is invalid no matter how crazy it may seem. Absolutely nothing. If someone tells you that you should be or think or feel a particular way, know that this is simply untrue. What you choose to do about your thoughts and feelings may be a choice, but any thoughts, feelings, and descriptions of experience should just be heard and validated as all part of your experience. Honor your experiences. At all times. Again, it is part of healing and empowerment.

Now, here's a third step that can be tricky, but is very important to healing and living from an empowered place. It's important that you are able to tell the trauma and drama and *find some positives*. Hear me out. Remember that I've said many times that there is nothing good about your child's medical issues. It's not a blessing in disguise, it's not something given to you so you can grow, it's not that you were chosen to handle these challenges for a reason. But it did happen to you just the same, so you may as well grow. You likely are growing. You can be empowered despite the extremes you have experienced. Most likely if you think really hard and deep (and this may take some work but will make all the difference), you can find some small and perhaps even big positives in your life. You're looking for evidence and examples that life is not just horrible and tragic.

An example: my patient, David, has a daughter who has dealt with an extended, very serious illness. She was only one year old when she was diagnosed, and very sick. There did not seem like there was anything good in their family for years. He felt like there was no reason to be happy, grateful, or see anything positive in life whatsoever.

On one particular day, when his daughter was about three years old, he went to retrieve the garbage pails from the street in front of his home. His daughter watched from the front door while he walked the ten yards to get the pails. When he turned back toward the home, he saw his bald-headed daughter smiling and waving. When he walked into the house, his daughter exclaimed "Daddy, I am so grown up, I didn't even worry while you were gone." David felt his daughter's strength at that moment and shared it as a positive moment that meant so much to him. He focused on searing that into his brain as well. It's a perspective that is bigger and goes beyond the tragic medical issue.

Any example can be a big or small positive. It could be something really big that happens that you could have never experienced if your child was not dealing with a medical issue. Watching your child help others, the way your child has become more compassionate, or even a funny story about something your child did or said, these can all be positives. Positives can come from many sources.

I recall feeling grateful and celebrating all green lights in NYC when we were headed home from one of my son's surgeries. It seemed like such a gift in that moment not to have to wait at red lights. He was in so much pain, and we just wanted to get him home as quickly as possible. It was going to be at least a two-hour trip. We made it in under an hour and a half. Nobody sails through NYC streets like that, ever.

So perhaps take a moment and take a breath and see if you can identify at least a few positives in your life, related or unrelated to your child. One possibility could even be that you are reading this now. That you are taking a moment for yourself. That is a positive. So, take a moment and see if you can generate some examples. The more the better. Write them down if you want. It will be good to have these examples to come back to at some point, particularly when you are feeling like life is one big negative mess.

Now here's the fourth step: when you are ready, take look at the challenges in your child's life and your life past or present, short-term, ongoing, or chronic. Is there something you could say about those challenges that is positive? Again, the challenges are awful and there is nothing positive in the suffering, but it's possible to say something positive nonetheless about what comes with the experience.

An example came from Sue, a child who has a chronic illness. She said she is here to teach others about the illness and show other kids that it's possible to be strong and courageous. Another child was able to start an awareness campaign and now sees it as her mission to bring awareness and funding for special programs for children and teens. These are what I call a BIG, BIG "miraculous level of positive goodness." We can't turn terrible things into rays of sunshine, but we can look for the "silver lining" – miraculous parts that appear at some point.

Your child's medical issue is in no way positive in and of itself. But there are gifts in the tragic challenges if you look for them. Seeing and honoring these gifts is crucial and empowering. It's where you can evolve and see the PTSD, and then also begin to make room for empowering post-traumatic growth. Challenges stretch us and we grow. We grow from pain. While it doesn't feel good to have the challenges, the growth is good. You can ask yourself, "Where am I now as a result of what I've been through?" And I mean besides all the pain, struggle, and exhaustion. I mean, what is in your life now that was not there before that you may feel grateful and fortunate to have in your life? This may take some work, but here are some more examples:

- the child who appreciates ice cream after not being able to eat much
- the parent who has greater appreciation for each moment in life and then appreciates a sunset
- the parent who is now more concerned about quality of time and less concerned about making money or what college their child attends
- the child who now wants to raise money and gets to be in the newspaper for his fundraising efforts

So really, really focusing on these positives, both big and small, leads you to the next and fifth step. The fifth step is what is referred to in my profession as neuroplasticity. It is basically the idea that the brain is not stuck or fixed and is more pliable than we previously thought. It means you can change the pathways in your brain. The more you practice breathing, seeing the positives, and creating more and more images and positive thoughts to practice, the more your brain starts to create alternative pathways. It will undermine the stuck, fixed, and traumatized brain and physiology in your body. The way it works is simple. Take a few deep breaths, think and picture positive thoughts and images, over and over and over, really focus on how great and empowering that feels. Breathe deep again.

Let's work through an example. Steven's son has a serious, life-threatening medical issue. His son has missed school, had multiple hospitalizations, and experiences great discomfort. The future is uncertain. Steven has felt great despair and often thinks that there is nothing good in life. Steven can only think initially about all the challenge and struggle. So Steven is asked to come up with a positive. After some time and thinking, Steven is able to see a small positive in the day he was on the phone with the health insurance company and was able to advocate for his child's healthcare coverage. This may seem like a small positive, but it is a positive. Dealing with the insurance company is the positive.

Next, Steven sees a BIG positive in his son's ability to tolerate annoying siblings. His son says to Steven's two other children, "You guys are ridiculous, who cares about those video games. You guys should realize there's more to life than video games."

Now, Steven could have just seen his children arguing and missed the gift of that moment. Instead, he saw how wise a comment his son had made about life. He saw that his son had a unique perspective for such a young person. Steven may not have seen that as a BIG positive or even missed it entirely if he had not been on the look-out for the unique miracles in his life. Steven then focused over and over on these images and events. Breathing and really taking in the positive feeling from these images and events.

Now, let's look at the sixth and last step, which is about ongoing practice and following up. It's important to keep practicing the breathing, positive focus, and repeated attention to positive images and thoughts. This practice will continue to set the stage for your brain to be making positive, healthy pathways for you. Ongoing practices, like any practice of breathing, meditation/imagery, and mindfulness, are something to do all the time, for the rest of your life. They apply to everything. They can make all the difference in how you experience and respond to any part of life.

Please also always seek support from others, including professionals, as needed. Use this book as a helpful tool and guide, but also speak with supportive groups if available or a fit once you have time, and seek professional counseling/ coaching with ongoing challenges and issues. There are often intensive recovery workshops and programs that you can attend for a day or weekend. Sometimes that can be a fit in a busy schedule that does not lend itself to regular, ongoing time commitments.

Yes, it's true that you, your child, and family will never be the same. It can be a strange swinging back and forth of thoughts and feelings. Perhaps you grieve the life you had prior to your child's medical issue, and yet somehow, you can embrace the amazing things that have come into your life as a result. Nothing good about the medical issue, and yet finding the good in it anyway.

This is a hero's journey of your own. A hero often combats adversity and through impressive feats is changed and then goes on to change the world. Every child that faces a serious or life-threatening medical issue is a hero. I often hear the term "warrior" in reference to children with ongoing serious illnesses. I hear countless stories even of children who do not survive, and yet make a difference in the world. Certainly they are all heroes, warriors, and miraculous beings. So are their parents. You are a hero, warrior, and amazing person too!

A Final Thought

"Hard times don't create heroes. It is during the hard times when the "hero" within us is revealed."
-Bob Riley

As I sat recently and watched my son swimming in the ocean waves, I noticed I was filled at the same moment with both joy and fear. It was a very intense experience of seemingly two opposing feelings. I see him at age 17, carefree and enjoying his time at the beach, and yet part of me was worried something horrible would happen to him in the water.

I was reminded that no matter what is happening and how good life may be going, I need to practice mindfulness. I need to fully allow and notice my experience without any judgment of the feelings, thoughts, and experiences. As I watched my son, I felt vulnerable and helpless, but then I also found a moment to be mindful and claim my empowered self. It was a choice.

In those moments on the beach, I thought to myself that I will continue to find my way in life, no matter what happens. There is always something within to hold onto, to get through any of life's challenges. It's true we never know what is in store for our lives and our child's life. We are never prepared for the anguish that accompanies our child facing a serious or life-threatening medical issue. We can know, however, that life is a mysterious, terrifying, and exciting journey filled with miracles, traumas, tragedies, and amazing power. Certainly to evolve and find our way is possible and yet not easy by any means. Embracing the life that is here and trusting yourself and your child's journey is certainly a choice that will allow some balance and wellness in the midst of crisis. It can also minimize any long-term effects of the stress you are experiencing.

Despite the feelings of vulnerability and helplessness, you are strong and empowered. It is always a choice to embrace that along the way. You can step into that empowered place at any time and claim it for yourself. You do not need to put yourself on hold. In fact, to do so is detrimental to yourself, your child, and family. I find taking a moment to breathe

(L.I.F.E.) and to see your strength and courage in these moments is supportive and energizing.

Your child is brave, courageous, and strong. You are a strong being, too. You are courageous and managing, even though it's not perfect. Please remember you can carry this with you in the center of your being at all times. Invite yourself to that highest level of living fully. To ride the waves and manage the storms in your life from an empowered place is an amazing gift for yourself and others around you. It doesn't change anything, and yet it changes everything. It's truly a lifeline... and so worth it!

Appendix I

Techniques and Strategies for Stress Management

1. Breathe deeply frequently. Use L.I.F.E breathing practice.
2. Essential oils. Lavender for calm and sleep, and citrus for mind-clearing and energy, as examples. You can place lavender on your pillow to promote sleep.
3. Acupressure. Apply light pressure to specific spots: the space between your eyes, ear lobes and entire outer ear, the space between thumb and forefinger on your hands, for example. Apply light pressure or gentle massage to each point for 30 seconds.
4. Professional acupuncture.
5. Drink water. Lots of water.
6. Massage. Professional or self-massage. Self-massage points such as neck, face, arms, legs, and feet. Rubbing and gently tapping various parts of your own body.

7. Stress-relieving foods including walnuts, pumpkin seeds, almonds, greens, blueberries, dark chocolate, salmon, garlic, oatmeal, avocado and citrus fruits.

8. Move your body in any way you can and get exercise if possible. Stretches. Lie flat on floor with bent knees to stretch out back/spine. Hang head over body by bending at your waist from a standing position to allow stress to flow out. Hold your elbows while in that upside down position. Try to walk around, even if you're stuck inside hospitals and treatment facilities. Use the stairs if possible, too.

9. Listen to music. Change the genre as needed. Sleep music for calm. Even upbeat music to dance and sing.

10. Listen to podcasts. Tara Brach, PhD, has many for free on her website as an example.

11. Watch programs, shows, and movies. Watching without commercials or recording so you can fast forward through commercials can be helpful.

12. Supplements, adrenal support/cortisol management type formulas, and rescue remedies (see Bach flower remedies and others in health food stores as an example).

13. Meditation. Silent, guided, or short one-minute meditations, for example. Even taking a brief

moment to feel your body in its space and notice your surroundings for 30 seconds.

14. Imagery. Practice using your images to create what is helpful and establish a sense of support and groundedness. An image of an anchor holding you in place could be an example.

15. Soak in bath with lavender oil and Epsom salt.

16. Humor. Watch comedy. Laugh at silly things. Find humor in the surprising places and laugh.

17. Talk to others about everything or anything OR decide at times not to talk, text, or stay in contact.

18. Permit yourself to do what fits without judging yourself.

19. Self-care and self-compassion practices. Spend even a moment appreciating and seeing yourself, honoring and loving yourself just the way you are.

20. Mindfulness. Stay in the moment, even just for the moment, without judgment.

21. Practice saying and focusing on positive perspective and seeing the gifts and strengths in you and your family. You are an amazing source of energy and courage, learning and evolving all the time.

Appendix II

What to Ask from Others While Dealing with a Child's Medical Issues

1. Just listen to me. Please just let me talk about whatever I want. You do not need to solve anything or try to say something in an attempt to make me feel better. Say, "I'm sorry this is going on," if anything. Tell me, "I'm here to talk, distract, laugh, or whatever fits for you right at the moment."

2. Please don't tell me you are sure everything will be ok. We don't know and I don't want to explain how serious this all is and that my child could die. Instead, say only that you can't imagine how difficult it is. Please say you know I'm strong and that you are sending us positive energy. Please don't say you "know" how it is for us.

3. Please don't say that you don't know how I'm managing everything that is going on for me and my

family. "I don't know how you do it" is not helpful. Instead you can say, "I see how strong you are and I admire you."

4. Please don't compare or tell me stories of other people you know that are dealing with a serious situation. It does not help. Instead, tell me you care about me and are there to support me and my family.

5. Please don't ask me to call you if I need something. I won't do that. I don't have time or energy sometimes to ask. Please make a specific offer. Offer to do an errand, bring over some food (check with me about this first, though, as I may have specific needs), drive my other children, come over to keep me company. Our needs change day to day, so please call and offer something specific. "I'm at the store right now, what can I get for you?" is a perfect example.

6. Don't tilt your head and look at me in pity. It makes me feel weak and awful. I love my child. There is no pity there.

7. Please ask about my child by name. Ask about what my child is doing and not just how they are doing with the medical issue. My child is more than their medical condition.

8. Please don't talk about me and my family to others in long conversations about what you all think may be going on. Nobody knows what it is like and it changes all the time. Instead say a prayer or some words that reflect positive energy.

9. Please don't assume I don't want to be bothered. I can decide what and when I want to be in contact. Don't take my lack of contact as anything personal.

10. Please try not to let fear drive you away from me and my family. Don't think that you have to stay away because it is too horrible. If it is too horrible and you can't cope with it, then that is fine. I'll figure that out and hold no grudge.

11. Laughing is fine even though it seems as there is nothing funny in my life. We do laugh. We do find humor in many places.

12. We are not "lucky" to take special trips or get gifts as a result of my child's medical issues. I would trade any trip or gift for my child's health.

13. Please don't feel badly about doing any of the things mentioned on this list. It's normal, understandable, and a common response. I did some of these things myself in the past.

14. We find joy and can see the miracle and gifts that my child has and brings to the world. Appreciate that and see that with us. My child is a gift and teaches us every day. My child is strong and courageous. We all can use a little more of that in our world.

Acknowledgements

O ne can hardly ever adequately thank everyone that helps make a book come into existence. I wrote this book for the parents of children with medical issues. I want to thank all the parents who face serious medical issues with a child. Your journey is unique. Out of pain and struggle has come amazing strength that has far-reaching power in the world. I hope I have done some of that justice in the words I offer to help.

To Bill O'Hanlon, author, therapist, coach, and songwriter, for his amazing guidance, instruction, support, and help in getting me crystal clear on my purpose, passion, topic, and so much more for the book.

To my publisher Angela Lauria, everyone at the Difference Press, my editor Maggie McReynolds, and all my fellow incubated authors, for what we experienced and shared together in order to make a difference with our messages in the world. Nobody other than Angela and Maggie could have made this book emerge out of me quite the way they did.

To my son's doctors and surgeons, especially Dr. Michael Kortbus, for excellent diagnosis, treatment, and helping us deal with those first days so well, Dr. Robert Ward and his surgical teams for the medical expertise that saved my son's life repeatedly and for going beyond to be kind and human, and to the nurses at NYU, especially Kate, who saved us over and over in so many ways.

To my family, friends, and colleagues who witnessed my struggle and stood by me through my son's illness, and then went on to support me to write this book, thank you for your sacrifices and for believing in me and my message.

To the people who may have not been able to be directly by my side and/or have helpful responses to me or my family, that was totally normal given the circumstances, and those moments actually became some of the most valuable experiences that informed me as I wrote this book.

And, to my husband Kevin, who witnessed and lived every moment with me and my son and then relived it all again and again and again. Thank you for your unending love and support in life and at every step needed for this book to be born.

About the Author

D r. Denise Morett is a psychologist with a private practice in the Hudson Valley of New York State, where she has practiced for over 25 years. She maintains a general psychology practice helping children, teens, and adults, and also consults at local hospitals, assisted living facilities, and nursing homes. Dr. Morett has treated patients with a full spectrum

Author's photo
courtesy of Carl Cox

of presenting issues inclusive of depression, anxiety, PTSD, bereavement, marital issues, childhood conditions, and families with a member facing a life-threatening or serious medical issue. She has lectured at universities and spoken to special interest groups as well as taught workshops and trainings.

Dr. Morett listens and provides a safe space as well as coping strategies for many patients and families with a member that has a serious or life-threatening medical issue. After 25 years of practice, she ironically found herself in those exact circumstances when her son was diagnosed with a very rare, life-threatening series of tumors. That began the most challenging, life-changing years of struggle. Driven by her wish for supportive information and coping strategies that were lacking, she provides the resources she needed at that time and learned in the years that followed. She is making a difference in the lives of children and families with her wish to use the lessons from both her professional experience and her life-changing firsthand personal experiences in order to help parents and families have at least one easier moment at the most unthinkable, unimaginable time in their lives.

Dr. Morett enjoys the moments in her life, more now than ever, and loves to boat on the Hudson River.

Thank You

LIFELINE could not have been written without all the brave parents and courageous children and families whose lives have been touched by a serious or life-threatening medical issue. It is my true wish for you that reading this book has made even the tiniest difference and helped you on some level. There are no easy answers or easy fixes, regardless of your circumstances and the outcomes of the medical issues. It's truly an honor to serve you and assist along the way. Life is changed in countless ways and hopefully you can connect to your own sense of empowerment and develop this even further within yourself. Hopefully you have found elements of *LIFELINE* useful and also developed and tailored this book to meet your needs and long term goals.

Residual and post-traumatic stress can endure and is most certainly an opportunity for growth. If we reprocess our experiences, they will settle in new and better ways so we can grow and not just be stuck in trauma. How can you know if you are ready to shift and find the wisdom and growth in yourself and your experiences? As an appreciation and honor to you, I have developed a quick tool to hone in on the exact stuck places and begin to learn to use them as a spring board for peace, wellness, and personal growth and evolution. Go to my website (parentingchildwithmedicalissues.com) and click on "LIFELINE toolkit."

Morgan James makes all of our titles available
through the Library for All Charity Organization.

www.LibraryForAll.org

CPSIA information can be obtained
at www.ICGtesting.com
Printed in the USA
BVHW03s1910160218
508365BV00001B/20/P